D1113380

God

can handle it...

for Graduates

God

can handle it…

for Graduates

Compiled and Edited by
Dr. Criswell Freeman

BRIGHTON BOOKS
Nashville, TN 37211
1-800-256-8584

ISBN 1-887655-96-4

The quoted ideas expressed in this book (but not scripture verses) are not, in all cases, exact quotations, as some have been edited for clarity and brevity. In all cases, the author has attempted to maintain the speaker's original intent. In some cases, quoted material for this book was obtained from secondary sources, primarily print media. While every effort was made to ensure the accuracy of these sources, the accuracy cannot be guaranteed. For additions, deletions, corrections or clarifications in future editions of this text, please write BRIGHTON BOOKS.

All scripture quotations, unless otherwise indicated, are taken from the HOLY BIBLE, NEW INTERNATIONAL VERSION ©, NIV ©, Copyright © 1973, 1978, 1984, by International Bible Society. Used by permission of Zondervan Publishing House. All rights reserved.

Scripture taken from *THE MESSAGE.* Copyright © 1993,1994,1995,1996. Used by permission of NavPress Publishing Group.

Printed in the United States of America
Layout by Sue Gerdes
Cover Design by Tal Howell
Typesetting by Criswell Freeman
1 2 3 4 5 6 7 8 9 10 • 99 00 01 02 03

ACKNOWLEDGMENTS
The author gratefully acknowledges the helpful support of Angela Freeman, Mary and Dick Freeman, and Jim Gallery.

For Guy Stewart Freeman and

All His Graduates

Table of Contents

A Message to Graduates 13

Chapter 1: God Can Handle It 15

Chapter 2: Your Partnership With God 31

Chapter 3: Keeping the Faith............................ 41

Chapter 4: The Work Ahead 57

Chapter 5: When Life Is Not Fair 71

Chapter 6: Love...83

Chapter 7: Hope 95

Chapter 8: Peace..105

Chapter 9: Courage..119

Chapter 10: Following God's Plan....................129

Chapter 11: It's a Wonderful Life.....................139

Quotations Indexed by Source.........................153

A Message to Graduates

Your graduation is a memorable occasion, one that will become a very important part of your personal history. Congratulations! As graduation approaches, you are undoubtedly preparing to embark upon your next great adventure. This book is designed to help.

After the sheepskin has been signed and framed, you will face countless opportunities and challenges. If you depend entirely upon your own judgement and resources, you will be disappointed. But if you form a partnership with God, if you learn to depend upon His power and not solely upon your own, you'll discover a reservoir of strength and comfort that will never run dry.

God has a plan for your life, but He won't force it upon you. Instead, God will wait patiently, never leaving your side for a moment. The instant that you reach out and accept His grace, your life will be changed forever. But reach out you must.

Your diploma will bear witness to countless hours of hard work, so enjoy every single minute of your graduation — you've earned it. But also take a few moments to consider the power-packed ideas in this little book. And remember that with God as your partner, there is nothing, absolutely nothing, that the two of you can't handle.

1

GOD CAN HANDLE IT

Graduation is an exciting time, a time of change, a time for new beginnings and, of course, a time for celebration. But graduation is not only a time for celebrating, it is also a wonderful time for contemplating. Amid all the pomp and circumstance, graduates are well-advised to save a few quiet moments for God.

Whether you realize it or not, God walks with you all day, every day. Graduation day is no different: God continues to work His plan for your life; it's your duty to listen to Him, read His Word, watch for His signs, and then conduct your life accordingly.

Catherine Marshall wrote, "God is trying to get a message through to you, and that message is simply this: 'Stop depending upon inadequate human resources. And let Me handle the matter.'" Graduates please take note: Whatever your plans, whatever your challenges, whatever your future may hold, God can handle it. So why not let Him?

God is the silent partner in all great enterprises.

Abraham Lincoln

Our Father in heaven, hallowed be your name,
your kingdom come, your will be done, on earth
as it is in heaven.
Matthew 6:9-10

Our labors are in vain unless God gives the Benediction.

Robert Herrick

...Always give yourselves fully to the work of the Lord, because you know that your labor in the Lord is not in vain.
I Corinthians 15:58

Every noble work is at first impossible.

Thomas Carlyle

Even now I am full of hope, but the end
lies in God.

Pindar

All heaven is waiting to help those
who will discover the will of God and do it.

J. Robert Ashcroft

*For we are God's fellow workers; you are
God's field, God's building.
I Corinthians 3:9*

God alone can finish.

John Ruskin

...Looking unto Jesus the author
and finisher of our faith.
Hebrews 12:1

One doesn't discover new lands without
consenting to lose sight of shore for
a very long time.

André Gide

To move the world, we must first
move ourselves.

Socrates

In God's faithfulness lies eternal security.

Corrie Ten Boom

...If God is for us, who can be against us?
Romans 8:31

God is the light of my darkness, the voice of my silence.

Helen Keller

God is light; in him there is no darkness at all.
I John 1:5

Fear not that your life shall come to an end,
but rather fear that it never has a beginning.
John Henry Cardinal Newman

If you love life, life will love you back.
Artur Rubinstein

The best way to prepare for life
is to begin to live.
Elbert Hubbard

Life is what we make it.
Always has been. Always will be.
Grandma Moses

Make a joyful noise unto the Lord, all ye lands.
Psalm 100:1 KJV

This is the day the Lord has made; let us rejoice and be glad in it.

Psalm 118:24

A day of worry is more exhausting than a day of work.

Sir John Lubbock

Therefore do not worry about tomorrow, for tomorrow will worry about itself. Each day has enough trouble of its own.
Matthew 6:34

A sad soul can kill you quicker than a germ.

John Steinbeck

Worry is interest paid on trouble
before it falls due.

William Ralph Inge

Man is what he believes.

Anton Chekhov

Despair is an evil counselor.

Sir Walter Scott

*Cast your cares on the Lord and
he will sustain you.
Psalm 55:22*

Worry often gives a small thing
a big shadow.

Swedish Proverb

Worry never robs tomorrow of its sorrow,
but only saps today of its strength.

A. J. Cronin

Worry is a state of mind based upon fear.

Napoleon Hill

*Even though I walk through the valley of the
shadow of death, I will fear no evil,
for you are with me....
Psalm 23:4*

"Worry" is a word I don't allow myself to use.

Dwight Eisenhower

He who fears the Lord has a secure fortress....
Proverbs 14:26

Faith can put a candle in
the darkest night.

Margaret Sangster

My God turns my darkness into light.
Psalm 18:28

Live from miracle to miracle.

Artur Rubinstein

*...With man this is impossible, but not with God;
all things are possible with God.
Mark 10:27*

Where God has put a period, do not change it to a question mark.

T. J. Bach

*Trust in the Lord with all thine heart; and lean
not unto thine own understanding.*
Proverbs 3:5 KJV

2

YOUR PARTNERSHIP
WITH GOD

As graduation nears, decisions must be made. Once the commencement speeches are concluded and the diplomas are dispensed, you'll be moving on to bigger and better things. You'll be making important plans for the future. Hopefully, those plans will include God.

God stands ready and willing to become your lifetime partner in every endeavor. He will counsel you in every important decision; He will be a source of strength during times of trouble; He will be a source of ceaseless joy — if you let Him. So do yourself this favor: Make God your partner in every aspect of life. He can handle it... and if you let Him, you'll be glad He did!

I have lived, Sir, a long time, and the longer I live, the more convincing proofs I see of this truth — that God governs in the affairs of men. And if a sparrow cannot fall to the ground without his notice, is it probable that an empire can rise without his aid?

Benjamin Franklin

Without the assistance of the Divine Being...I cannot succeed. With that assistance I cannot fail!

Abraham Lincoln

The Lord is near to all who call on him....
Psalm 145:18

God does not die on the day
when we cease to believe in a personal deity,
but we die on the day when our lives cease to
be illumined by the steady radiance,
of a wonder, the source of which
is beyond all reason.

Dag Hammarskjöld

God never tells us what he is going to do;
he reveals who he is.

Oswald Chambers

God is the beyond in the midst of our lives.

Dietrich Bonhoeffer

*The Lord is near. Do not be
anxious about anything....
Philippians 4:5-6*

I never really look
for things. I accept
whatever God throws
my way. Whichever way
God turns my feet,
that's the way I go.

Pearl Bailey

*If the Lord delights in a man's way, he makes
his steps firm; though he stumble, he will not fall,
for the Lord upholds him with his hand.
Psalm 37:23-24*

God can do more without us than we can do without him.

Meister Eckhart

Hath not the potter power over the clay?
Romans 9:21 KJV

Whatever we leave to God, God does...and blesses us.

Henry David Thoreau

*...I know whom I believed, and am convinced
that he is able to guard what I have entrusted to
him for that day.
2 Timothy 1:12*

Life is God's novel. Let him write it.

Isaac Bashevis Singer

With them I gladly shared my all and
learned the great truth that where
God guides, he provides.

Frank Buchman

God gives us always strength enough,
and sense enough, for everything he
wants us to do.

John Ruskin

...if it be of God, ye cannot overthrow it....
Acts 5:39 KJV

Let us bring what is our own. God will supply the rest.

Saint John Chrysostom

The Lord is my shepherd, I shall not want.
Psalm 23:1

Begin to weave and God will give the thread.

German Proverb

*Commit thy works unto the Lord...the Lord hath
made all things....
Proverbs 16:3-4 KJV*

Have courage for the
great sorrows of life and
patience for the small
ones; and when you have
laboriously accomplished
your daily task, go to
sleep in peace.
God is awake.

Victor Hugo

*Come to me, all you who are weary and
burdened, and I will give you rest.
Matthew 11:28*

3

KEEPING THE FAITH

Graduation day is a happy day filled with good feelings all around. But all days are not so cheerful. When tough times arrive, as they sometimes do, all of us, graduates and non-graduates alike, need faith.

The words on these pages remind us of the importance of a firm, committed faith in God, a faith that will serve us in good times and bad. Graduation day, or any other day for that matter, is the perfect day to renew that faith.

Faith is an activity; it is something
that has to be applied.

Corrie Ten Boom

Faith is kept alive in us, and
gathers strength, more from practice
than from speculations.

Joseph Addison

He does not believe who does not live
according to his beliefs.

Thomas Fuller

...I will show you my faith by what I do.
James 2:18

True faith is never found alone; it is accompanied by expectation.

C. S. Lewis

Blessed are those who have not seen and yet have believed.
John 20:29

Never despair,
but if you do,
work on in despair.

Edmund Burke

Blessed is the man who perseveres under trial.
James 1:12

Adopt the pace of nature. Her secret is patience.

Ralph Waldo Emerson

It is good that a man should both hope and quietly wait for the salvation of the Lord.
Lamentations 3:25 KJV

Adversity is the first path to truth.

Byron

There is no education like adversity.

Benjamin Disraeli

God will not look you over for medals,
degrees or diplomas, but for scars.

Elbert Hubbard

Be strong and courageous. Do not be afraid or
terrified because of them for the Lord your God
goes with you; he will never leave you
nor forsake you.
Deuteronomy 31:6

Human adversity is too great for man to live without faith.

Heinrich Heine

In this world you will have trouble. But take heart! I have overcome the world.
John 16:33

The only limit to our realization of tomorrow
will be our doubts of today. Let us move
forward with strong and active faith.

Franklin D. Roosevelt

Faith is not believing that God can,
but that God will!

Abraham Lincoln

Faith is the antiseptic of the soul.

Walt Whitman

*We wait in hope for the Lord; he is our help
and our shield.*
Psalm 33:20

Alas! The fearful unbelief
is unbelief in yourself.

Thomas Carlyle

Fear knocked at the door. Faith answered.
No one was there.

Inscription, Hind's Head Inn, Bray, England

Nothing is impossible to a willing heart.

John Heywood

*...Because you have so little faith I tell you the
truth, if you have faith as small as a mustard
seed, you can say to this mountain, "Move from
here to there," and it will move.
Nothing will be impossible for you.
Matthew 17:20*

Great hopes make great men.

Thomas Fuller

Hope thou in God.
Psalm 42:5 KJV

 W e see things as we are,
              not as they are.

Leo Rosten

 O ptimism is the faith that leads
      to achievement. Nothing can be done
         without hope and confidence.

Helen Keller

 D ear Lord, never let me be afraid
         to pray for the impossible.

Dorothy Shellenberger

Is anything too hard for the Lord?
Genesis 18:14

Doubt is a pain too lonely
to know that faith is
his twin brother.

Kahlil Gibran

Some things have to be believed
to be seen.

Ralph Hodgson

We never test the resources of God until
we attempt the impossible.

F. B. Meyer

In the Lord I put my trust....
Psalm 11:1

Faith dares the soul to go farther than it can see.

William Newton Clark

...stand firm in the faith; be men of courage;
be strong.
I Corinthians 16:13

The primary cause of unhappiness in
the world today is...lack of faith.

Carl Jung

When we lose God,
it is not God who is lost.

Anonymous

Faith is the force of life.

Leo Tolstoy

...thy faith hath made thee whole;
go in peace....
Mark 5:34 KJV

Faith is not something to grasp;
it is a state to grow into.

Gandhi

The principle part of faith is patience.

George Mac Donald

Faith is God's work within us.

Saint Thomas Aquinas

...My grace is sufficient for you.
2 Corinthians 12:9

When I learned to practice mustard-seed faith and positive thinking, remarkable things happened.

Sir John Walton

*The fundamental fact of existence is that this
trust in God, this faith, is the firm foundation
under everything that makes life worth living.
It's our handle on what we can't see.
Hebrews 11:1 THE MESSAGE*

4

THE WORK AHEAD

Graduation is a time to reflect upon the past and plan for the future. A signed diploma is ample evidence of your past successes. But what about the work ahead? God has something to say about that.

God does not promise that your life's work will be easy; He does not promise that the rewards will be quick. But God does give His assurance that if you do His work here on earth, you will earn more blessings than you can count.

As you make plans for your life's work, be sure to include God in those plans. With God by your side, the work ahead, whatever form it takes, will be meaningful, and your rewards will be heavenly.

Oh Lord, Thou givest us everything at the price of effort.

Leonardo da Vinci

Whatsoever thy hand findeth to do,
do it with thy might.
Ecclesiastes 9:10 KJV

Call on God, but row
away from the rocks.

Ralph Waldo Emerson

Be bold.
Have the will to do,
The soul to dare.

Sir Walter Scott

The things, good Lord, that I pray for,
give me thy grace to labor for.

Sir Thomas More

*As long as it is day, we must do the work of him
who sent me. Night is coming when
no one can work.*
John 9:4

There is a future
that makes itself
and a future we make.
The real future
is composed
of both.

Alain

Whatsoever ye do in word or deed,
do all in the name of Lord Jesus....
Colossians 3:17

Action springs not from thought,
but from a readiness for responsibility.

Dietrich Bonhoeffer

The smallest actual good is better than
the most magnificent promises
of impossibilities.

Thomas Macaulay

The only measure of what you believe is
what you do. If you want to know what people
believe, don't read what they write, don't ask
them what they believe, just observe
what they do.

Ashley Montagu

*He shall reward every man
according to his works.
Matthew 16:27*

In creating, the only hard thing
is to begin.

James Russell Lowell

He who has begun is half done.
Dare to be wise: Begin!

Horace

The beginning is the most important part
of the work.

Plato

The day is short, the labor long,
the workers are idle, the reward is great,
and the Master is urgent.

Rabbi Tarfon

*...Anyone who has faith in me will do what
I have been doing. He will do
greater things than these....
John 14:12*

Facing it,
always facing it,
that's the way
to get through.

Joseph Conrad

*The Lord is the strength of my life;
of whom shall I be afraid?
Psalm 27:1*

All work is a seed sown: It grows and spreads and sows itself anew.

Thomas Carlyle

Remember this: Whoever sows sparingly shall reap sparingly and whoever sows generously shall reap generously.
2 Corinthians 9:6

Blessed is the man who has
found his work.

Elbert Hubbard

Work is not a curse,
it is a blessing from God.

Pope John Paul II

Work as if you were to live a hundred years;
pray as if you were to die tomorrow.

Ben Franklin

Our greatest weariness comes
from work not done.

Eric Hoffer

Be rich in good works.
1 Timothy 6:18 KJV

Nothing is really work unless
you'd rather be doing something else.

Sir James Barrie

The more I want to get something done,
the less I call it work.

Richard Bach

Work for your soul's sake.

Edgar Lee Masters

When your work speaks for itself,
don't interrupt.

Henry Kaiser

...The labourer is worthy of his reward.
1 Timothy 5:18 KJV

God gives every bird its food, but he does not throw it into the nest.

Josiah Gilbert Holland

...if any would not work, neither should he eat.
2 Thessalonians 3:10 KJV

To the worker God himself lends aid.

Euripides

God gives talent.
Work transforms talent into genius.

Anna Pavlova

What you are is God's gift to you.
What you make of it is your gift to God.

Anthony Dalla Villa

...each man has his own gift from God....
I Corinthians 4:7

Each person's life is a portrait of himself.

Samuel Butler

It is easier to do a job right than
to explain why you didn't.

Martin Van Buren

When love and skill work together,
expect a masterpiece.

John Ruskin

*...my judgment is with the Lord, and
my work with my God.
Isaiah 49: 4 KJV*

Believe in the Lord and he will do half the work ... the last half.

Cyrus Curtis

Whatever you do, work at it with all your heart as working for the Lord, not for men....
Colossians 3:23

5

WHEN LIFE IS NOT FAIR

Life does not always seem fair, because we mortals are unable to see the totality of God's plans. God's ways surpass human understanding, and try as we might, we simply can't fathom the boundaries of His work. Like it or not, we must live with the faith that God knows exactly what He's doing, even when we don't.

When you face adversity or when you suffer loss, you may be tempted to fall into despair. Not so fast! God can handle it, if you let Him.

When life seems unfair, don't spend too much time asking "Why?" Instead, ask God "What next?" Then get busy, because His plan for you is more beautiful than you can imagine.

Worry and anxiety are sand in the
    machinery of life; faith is the oil.

E. Stanley Jones

No matter what happens to you,
    if you can draw strength from God
    and the people you love,
    nothing can ever defeat you.

Reba McEntire

Anxiety is the great modern plague.
    But faith can cure it.

Smiley Blanton, M.D.

Let not your heart be troubled; believe in God,
believe also in me.
John 14:1 KJV

Difficulties are God's errands and trainers, and only through them can one come to the fullness of humanity.

Henry Ward Beecher

A man's wisdom gives him patience.
Proverbs 19:11

God allows us to experience the low points of life in order to teach us lessons we could learn in no other way.

C.S. Lewis

I sought the Lord, and he answered me;
he delivered me from all my fears.
Psalm 34:4

Obstacles are those frightful things you see when you take your eyes off the goal.

Hannah More

I will lift up mine eyes unto the hills, from whence cometh my help.
Psalm 121:1 KJV

The greatest part of our happiness and misery depends on our dispositions and not our circumstances.

Martha Washington

I have learned to be content whatever the circumstances…
Philippians 4:11

Strengthen yourself with contentment,
for it is an impregnable fortress.

Epictetus

God give me the serenity to accept
the things which cannot be changed;
Give me the courage to change things
which must be changed;
And give me the wisdom to distinguish
one from the other.

Reinhold Niebuhr

In His will is our peace.

Dante

Cast thy burden upon the Lord,
and he shall sustain thee.
Psalm 55:22 KJV

The saints are sinners who keep on going.

R. L. Stevenson

*I waited patiently for the Lord; he turned to me
and heard my cry.
Psalm 40:1*

Life is not in holding a good hand
but in playing a poor hand well.

Unknown

Time deals gently only with those who
take it gently.

Anatole France

Life does not have to be perfect
to be wonderful.

Annette Funicello

I know God will not give me anything
I cannot handle. I just wish He didn't
trust me so much.

Mother Teresa

He will not fail thee, or forsake thee.
Deuteronomy 31:6

Prudence dictates to us to make the best
we can of inevitable evils. We may fret and
fume and peeve and scold and rave,
but what good does it do?

John Adams

God asks no man whether he will accept life.
That is not the choice. You must take it.
The only choice is how.

Henry Ward Beecher

There is only one way to happiness and that
is to cease worrying about things that are
beyond the power of our will.

Epictetus

*...Thy will be done in earth,
as it is in heaven.
Matthew 6:10 KJV*

The man who has become emancipated
from the empire of worry will find life a much
more cheerful affair than it used to be while
he was perpetually being irritated.

Bertrand Russell

If you haven't the strength to impose your
own terms upon life, you must accept
the terms it offers you.

T. S. Eliot

True peace is found by man in the depths
of his own heart, the dwelling place of God.

Johannes Tauler

*The Lord is my rock, my fortress and my
deliverer; my God is my rock,
in whom I take refuge.
Psalm 18:2*

The secret of happiness
is to cease worrying
about things that are
beyond our power
to control.

Epictetus

*...I have learned the secret of being content in
any and every situation, whether well fed or
hungry, whether living in plenty or in want.
Philippians 4:12*

6

LOVE

Because you have graduated, you've obviously earned passing grades in the classroom. Congratulations! But to earn passing grades in the bigger classroom known as "the real world," you must first learn to follow God's instructions concerning love. Without love, there can be no passing grades, but with enough love, failure is impossible.

God has given us clear instructions concerning the way that we are to treat others. As in all earthly matters, God has the final say; and when it comes to human relations, God's final word is "love." Period.

When the evening of this life comes, we shall be judged on love.

St. John of the Cross

For God so loved the world that he gave his one and only Son, that whoever believes in him shall not perish but have eternal life.
John 3:16

Nothing we do, however virtuous,
    can be accomplished alone; therefore
        we are saved by love.

Reinhold Niebuhr

Love is that splendid triggering of
human vitality...the supreme activity which
nature affords anyone for going out of
himself toward someone else.

Ortega y Gasset

Love is the only sane and satisfactory
answer to the problem of human existence.

Erich Fromm

...the fruit of the spirit is love....
Galatians 5:22

Love is too large, too deep ever to be truly
understood or measured or limited within
the framework of words.

M. Scott Peck

In our life there is a single color, as on an
artist's palette, which provides
the meaning of life and art.
It is the color of love.

Marc Chagall

It is not love, but lack of love, which is blind.

Glenway Wescott

*Be completely humble and gentle; be patient,
bearing with one another in love.
Ephesians 4:2*

It is love that seeks, that knocks,
that finds, and that is faithful
to what it finds.

Saint Augustine

A man is not where he lives,
but where he loves.

Latin Proverb

Love is the everlasting possession
of the good.

Plato

...Love your neighbor as yourself.
Matthew 19:19

Bitterness imprisons life;
love releases it.
Bitterness paralyzes life;
love empowers it.

Harry Emerson Fosdick

*By this all men will know you are my disciples,
if you love one another.
John 13:35*

Love is an act of endless forgiveness,
a tender look which becomes a habit.

Peter Ustinov

Forgiveness is God's command.

Martin Luther

Love wins when everything else will fail.

Fanny Jackson Coppin

To err is human; to forgive, divine.

Alexander Pope

Forgive as the Father forgave you.
Colossians 3:13

Life is the flower of which love is the honey.

Victor Hugo

And now these three remain: faith, hope, and love. But the greatest of these is love.
1 Corinthians 13:13

All who would win joy must share it; happiness was born a twin.

Lord Byron

[Love] keeps no record of wrongs.
1 Corinthians 13:5

Love is the crowning grace of humanity,
the holiest right of the soul.

Petrarch

Love is a multiplication.

Marjory Stoneman Douglas

To be loved, love.

Decimus Maximus Ausonius

*Be kind and compassionate to one another,
forgiving each other, just as in Christ
God forgave you.
Ephesians 4:32*

Love is the essence of God.

Ralph Waldo Emerson

Everyone who loves has been born of God and knows God. Whoever does not love does not know God, because God is love.
1 John 4:7-8

Where love is, there is God also.

Leo Tolstoy

*God is love. Whoever lives in love
lives in God, and God in him.
1 John 4:16*

7

HOPE

Graduation day is a time to bask in the glory. Whatever you do, cherish this wonderful moment. But it's never too early to prepare yourself for a day in the not-too-distant future when you may encounter Old Man Trouble. If you do, remember this important truth: Your attitude toward the future will determine, in large part, how your future unfolds.

God is merciful; all of us can take comfort in this fact. As long as we hold out hope, there is hope for us. As long as we keep the faith, the faith will keep us. And as long as we expect miracles, God will continue to amaze us with the glory of His works.

No matter your circumstances, expect the best and let God handle the rest. Just keep working and keep trusting in God. Do today's work and don't worry too much about tomorrow. The future, for those who trust in the Lord, has a way of taking care of itself.

They can conquer who believe they can.

Ralph Waldo Emerson

*Everything is possible
for him who believes.
Mark 9:23*

Act as though it were impossible to fail.

Dorthea Brand

Trust in him at all times....
Psalm 62:8

Hope, like faith, is nothing if it is not courageous.

Thornton Wilder

Happy is he that hath the God of Jacob for his help, whose hope is in the Lord his God.
Psalm 146:5 KJV

Hope is a thing with feathers
     that perches in the soul.

Emily Dickinson

The future belongs to those
  who believe in the beauty of their dreams.

Eleanor Roosevelt

Belief in a thing makes it happen.

Frank Lloyd Wright

*Hope deferred maketh the heart sick: but when
the desire cometh, it is a tree of life.
Proverbs 13:12 KJV*

God's gifts put man's best dreams
to shame.

Elizabeth Barrett Browning

In the presence of hope, faith is born.

Robert Schuller

Sad soul, take comfort nor forget,
The sunrise never failed us yet.

Celia Thaxter

Joy comes in the morning.
Psalm 30:5

Cast your cares on the
Lord and he will
sustain you.

Psalm 55:22

Aim at heaven and you will get earth thrown in. Aim at earth and you will get neither.

C. S. Lewis

*…for I am your God. I will strengthen you
and help you….*
Isaiah 41:10

It is not well for a man to pray cream and live skim milk.

Henry Ward Beecher

Ask and it will be given to you; seek and you will find; knock and the door will be opened to you.
Matthew 7:7

God's in his heaven,
All's right with the world!

Robert Browning

The heavens declare his righteousness,
and all the people see his glory.
Psalm 97:6

8

PEACE

When the diploma is safely signed and framed, most graduates feel a sense of accomplishment and peace. But the warm feeling of a signed sheepskin pales in comparison to the profound sense of peace that comes from a right relationship with God.

God offers us "peace that passes understanding." It is, of course, up to each of us to accept that divine peace offering. The words on the following pages show us how.

The mind is its own place, and in itself can
make a heaven of hell, a hell of heaven.

John Milton

A happy life consists in tranquillity of mind.

Cicero

The mind is never right but when it is
at peace within itself.

Lucius Annaeus Seneca

...Seek peace and pursue it.
Psalm 34:14

We have peace with God through our Lord Jesus Christ.

Paul the Apostle

Peace I leave with you. My peace I give you. I do not give to you as the world gives. Do not let your hearts be troubled and do not be afraid.
John 14:27

True peace is found by man in the depths
of his own heart, the dwelling place of God.

Johannes Tauler

Be good, keep your feet dry,
your eyes open, your heart at peace
and your soul in the joy of Christ.

Thomas Merton

*...we know that in all things God works for the
good of those who love him....*
Romans 8:28

Great men are they who see that spiritual force is stronger than material force.

Ralph Waldo Emerson

*Blessed God! His love is
the wonder of the world.
Psalm 31:21*

A man's life is
what his thoughts make of it.
Marcus Aurelius

All that a man does outwardly is
but the expression and completion of his
inward thought. To work effectively,
he must think clearly; to act nobly,
he must think nobly.
William Ellery Channing

*Finally, brothers, whatever is true, whatever is
noble, whatever is right, whatever is pure,
whatever is lovely, whatever is admirable...
think about such things.*
Philippians 4:8

Find the journey's end in every step.

Ralph Waldo Emerson

The steps of a good man are ordered by the Lord.
Psalm 37:23

God is our refuge and strength, an ever-present help in trouble.

Psalm 46:1

I will lift up mine eyes
unto the hills, from
whence cometh my help.
My help cometh from
the Lord which made
heaven and earth.

Psalm 121:1-2 KJV

I will not meddle with that which
I cannot mend.

Thomas Fuller

Acceptance makes any new event
put on a new face.

G. K. Chesterton

There are two kinds of people:
those who say to God, "Thy will be done,"
and those to whom God says, "All right,
then, have it your way."

C. S. Lewis

...not my will, but thine, be done.
Luke 22:42

The world is a looking glass and gives back to
every man the reflection of his own face.
Frown at it and it will in turn look sourly
upon you; laugh at it and with it,
and it is a jolly, kind companion.

William Makepeace Thackeray

Laugh and the world laughs with you.
Weep and you weep alone.

Ella Wheeler Wilcox

The clearest sign of wisdom is
continued cheerfulness.

Michel de Montaigne

Worship the Lord with gladness.
Psalm 100:2

Cast away care; he that loves sorrow lengthens not a day, nor can he buy tomorrow.

Thomas Dekker

He replied, "You of little faith, why are you so afraid?" Then he got up and rebuked the winds and the waves, and it was completely calm.
Matthew 8:26

Of all the gifts bestowed on human beings, hearty laughter must be close to the top.

Norman Cousins

*There is a time for everything...a time to weep
and a time to laugh....
Ecclesiastes 3:1,4*

When you cannot sleep at night, stop counting sheep and talk to the shepherd.

Unknown

*I will lie down and sleep in peace, for you alone,
O Lord, make me dwell in safety.
Psalm 4:8*

9

COURAGE

Graduation means that it's time for big changes in your life. Soon, you will be leaving the safety of a familiar environment and embarking upon the next stage of your own personal adventure. This change can be unsettling, but fear not: Wherever you go, God is there.

This graduation is simply preparation for many more that will come. Throughout life, you will make many transitions. As you face the realities of an uncertain future, God can serve as an ever-present source of courage and strength.

As you consider the words that follow, remember that life is full of graduations; some formal, some informal. And remember that every time you graduate from one stage of life to another, God attends the ceremony...and smiles.

Courage

Never take counsel of your fears.

Andrew Jackson

Courage is contagious.
When a brave man takes a stand,
the spines of others are often stiffened.

Billy Graham

One man with courage is a majority.

Andrew Jackson

When in doubt, do the courageous thing.

Jan Smuts

Be brave. Be strong. Don't give up.
Expect God to get here soon.
Psalm 31:24 THE MESSAGE

Courage can achieve everything.

Sam Houston

The Lord is my light and my salvation—
whom shall I fear?
The Lord is the stronghold of my life—
of whom shall I be afraid?
Psalm 27:1

Courage

They conquer who believe they can.
He has not learned the first lesson of life
who does not every day surmount a fear.

Ralph Waldo Emerson

Pray not for safety from danger,
but for deliverance from fear.

Ralph Waldo Emerson

Courage is resistance to fear,
mastery of fear, not absence of fear.

Mark Twain

Courage is being scared to death
but saddling up anyway.

John Wayne

*Now Lord...enable your servants to speak your
word with great boldness.
Acts 4:29*

Never surrender opportunity to security.

Branch Rickey

The desire for safety stands against
every great and noble enterprise.

Tacitus

Become so wrapped up in something
that you forget to be afraid.

Lady Bird Johnson

Never let the fear of striking out
get in your way.

Babe Ruth

*...Act with courage, and may the Lord be with
those who do well.
2 Chronicles 19:11*

Courage is the price life extracts for granting peace.

Amelia Earhart

...Why are ye fearful,
O ye of little faith?
Matthew 8:26 KJV

Keep your conscience clear, then never fear.

Poor Richard's Almanac

Be strong and very courageous. Be careful to obey all the law...
Joshua 1:7

Courage

Fear always springs from ignorance.

Ralph Waldo Emerson

He who fears he shall suffer
already suffers what he fears.

Michel de Montaigne

Do the thing you fear
and the death of fear is certain.

Ralph Waldo Emerson

*Though I walk in the midst of trouble, you
preserve me...with your right hand
you save me.
Psalm 138:7*

Courage is not simply one of the virtues, but the form of every virtue at the testing point.

C. S. Lewis

Be faithful, even to the point of death, and I will give you the crown of life.
Revelation 2:10

You gain strength, courage and confidence by every experience in which you stop to look fear in the face.

Eleanor Roosevelt

...Be strong and of a good courage; be not afraid, neither be thou dismayed: for the Lord thy God is with thee....
Joshua 1:9 KJV

10

FOLLOWING GOD'S PLAN

As you come face-to-face with life after graduation, you will begin making plans. And as you plan for the future, remember to include God.

Horace Bushnell wrote, "Every man's life is a plan of God." Your life is no exception. If you seek the abundance and joy that only God can give, you must be willing to share your future with Him.

As you plan for your postgraduate work, seek God's counsel. Keep searching for His will in your life. Remember that while it's important to make plans for your future, it's much more important to understand that God, too, has a plan — a perfect plan — for you.

God's heavenly plan doesn't always make earthly sense.

Charles Swindoll

For I know the plans I have for you…
plans to prosper you.
Jeremiah 29:11

Give to us clear vision that we may know
where to stand and what to stand for —
because unless we stand for something,
we shall fall for anything.

Peter Marshall

Cure yourself of the condition of bothering
about how you look to other people. Concern
yourself only with how you appear to God.

Miguel de Unamuno

The strength and happiness of a man
consists in finding out the way in which
God is going, and going in that way too.

Henry Ward Beecher

...Wisdom is proved right by her actions.
Matthew 11:19

Following God's Plan

I want what God wants;
        that is why I am so merry.

Saint Francis of Assisi

The center of God's will is our only safety.

Corrie Ten Boom

To walk out of his will is to walk
        into nowhere.

C. S. Lewis

We wait in hope for the Lord;
he is our help and our shield.
Psalm 33:43

God reveals himself unfailingly to the thoughtful seeker.

Honoré de Balzac

*But the plans of the Lord stand firm forever,
the purposes of his heart through
all generations.
Psalm 33:11*

Make your life a mission ...
>> not an intermission.

Arnold Glasgow

Life is either a daring adventure or nothing.

Helen Keller

If I were to wish for anything,
>> I should not wish for wealth and power,
>>> but for the passionate sense
>>> of the potential.

Kierkegaard

...what does the Lord your God ask of you...to serve the Lord your God with all your heart and with all your soul.
Deuteronomy 10:12

Live out your life in its full meaning; it is God's life.

Josiah Royce

For none of us lives to himself alone....
Whether we live or die,
we belong to the Lord.
Romans 14:7-8

It is not death that a man should fear, but he should fear never beginning to live.

Marcus Aurelius

To every thing there is a season, and a time to every purpose under heaven: a time to be born, and a time to die....
Ecclesiastes 3:1-2

Do not walk through time without leaving worthy evidence of your passage.

Pope John XXIII

This is to my Father's glory, that you bear much fruit, showing yourselves to be my disciples.
John 15:8

The will of God will not take you where the grace of God cannot keep you.

Unknown

The Lord will fulfill his purpose for me; your love, O Lord, endures forever....
Psalm 138:8

11

IT'S A WONDERFUL LIFE

This book, like your graduation ceremony, must now come to an end. We conclude with a celebration of God's wonderful and mysterious gift: the gift of life.

As you consider the verses and quotations in this final chapter, remember that your life is a priceless treasure on loan from God; so make the most of it. Live each day to the fullest, seek God's will, stay humble, and give thanks for the blessings you've been given. And remember that as long as you keep God in your heart, it's a wonderful life.

Write on your heart that every day is
the best day of the year.

Ralph Waldo Emerson

Each day provides its own gifts.

Martial

To him whose elastic and vigorous thought
keeps pace with the sun,
the day is a perpetual morning.

Henry David Thoreau

The heavens declare the glory of God.
Psalm 19:1

Life is a journey,
not a destination.
Happiness is not "there"
but here, not "tomorrow"
but today.

Sidney Greenberg

*I know that there is nothing better for men than
to be happy and do good while they live.
Ecclesiastes 3:12*

Nobody's gonna live for you.

Dolly Parton

Tomorrow's life is too late. Live today.

Martial

Brief is the space allotted to you;
     pass it as pleasantly as you can,
        not grieving from noon to eve.

Euripides

...a cheerful heart fills the day with song...
Proverbs 15:15 THE MESSAGE

A grateful mind is a great mind which
eventually attracts to itself great things.

Plato

You are today where your thoughts
have brought you; you will be tomorrow
where your thoughts take you.

James Lane Allen

So it is of cheerfulness:
The more it is spent, the more of it remains.

Ralph Waldo Emerson

A merry heart doeth good like a medicine:
but a broken spirit drieth bones.
Proverbs 17:22 KJV

I will not just live my life.
I will not just spend my life.
I will invest my life.

Helen Keller

*Instruct them to do good, to be rich in good
works, to be generous and
ready to share.
1 Timothy 6:18 NASB*

Don't mistake pleasure for happiness.

Josh Billings

*Follow the steps of the Godly instead and stay
on the right path for only good men
enjoy life to the full.
Proverbs 2:20*

Each day provides its own gifts.

Martial

Anyone who keeps the ability to see beauty never grows old.

Franz Kafka

Joy is the simplest form of gratitude.

Karl Barth

Know ye that the Lord he is God. It is he that hath made us, and not we ourselves; we are his people and the sheep of his pasture.
Psalm 100:3 KJV

Time is so precious that God deals it out only second by second.

Bishop Fulton J. Sheen

The Lord formed man of the dust of the ground, and breathed into his nostrils the breath of life.
Genesis 2:7 KJV

May you live all the days of your life.

Jonathan Swift

*Blessed are those whose strength is in you, who
have set their hearts on pilgrimage.
Psalm 84:5*

No matter how long you live, die young.

Elbert Hubbard

Never be lacking in zeal, but keep your spiritual fervor, serving the Lord.
Romans 12:11

Give thanks to Him and praise his name. For the Lord is good and his love endures forever; his faithfulness continues through all generations.

Psalm 100: 4-5

Quotations Indexed By Source

Quotations Indexed by Source

Adams, John 80
Addison, Joseph 42
Alain 60
Allen, James Lane 143
Aquinas, Saint Thomas 55
Ashcroft, Robert 18
Augustine 87
Bach, Richard 66
Bach, T. J. 30
Bailey, Pearl 34
Balzac, Honore' de 133
Barrie, Sir James 66
Barth, Karl 146
Beecher, Henry Ward
    73, 80, 103, 131
Billings, Josh 145
Blanton, Smiley 72
Bonhoeffer, D. 33, 61
Boom, Corrie Ten
    20, 42, 132
Brand, Dorthea 97
Browning, Elizabeth
    Barrett 100
Browning, Robert 104
Buchman, Frank 37
Burke, Edmund 44
Bushnell, Horace 129
Butler, Samuel 69
Byron 46, 91
Carlyle, Thomas
    18, 49, 64
Chagall, Marc 86

Chambers, Oswald 33
Channing, William Ellery
    110
Chekhov, Anton 25
Chesterton, G. K. 114
Chrysostom, Saint John 38
Cicero 106
Clark, William Newton 53
Conrad, Joseph 63
Coppin, Fanny Jackson 89
Cousins, Norman 117
Cronin, A. J. 26
Curtis, Cyrus 70
Dante 77
Decimus Maximus
    Ausonius 92
Dekker, Thomas 116
Dickinson, Emily 99
Disraeli, Benjamin 46
Douglas, Marjory
    Stoneman 92
Earhart, Amelia 124
Eckhart, Meister 35
Eisenhower, Dwight 27
Eliot, T. S. 81
Emerson, Ralph Waldo
    45, 59, 93, 96, 109, 111,
    122, 126, 140, 143
Epictetus 77, 80, 82
Euripides 68, 142
Fosdick, Harry Emerson
    88

France, Anatole 79
Franklin, Ben 32. 65
Fromm, Erich 85
Fuller, T. 42, 50, 114
Funicello, Annette 79
Gandhi 55
Gibran, Kahlil 52
Gide, André 20
Glasgow, Arnold 134
Graham, Billy 120
Greenberg, Sidney 141
Hammarskjöld, Dag 33
Heine, Heinrich 47
Herrick, Robert 17
Heywood, John 49
Hill, Napoleon 26
Hodgson, Ralph 52
Hoffer, Eric 65
Holland, Josiah Gilbert 67
Horace 62
Houston, Sam 121
Hubbard, Elbert
    22, 46, 65, 149
Hugo, Victor 40, 90
Inge, William Ralph 25
Jackson, Andrew 120
Johnson, Lady Bird 123
Jones, E. Stanley 72
Jung, Carl 54
Kafka, Franz 146
Kaiser, Henry 66
Keller, H. 21, 51, 134, 144

Kierkegaard 134
Leonardo da Vinci 58
Lewis, C. S.
    43, 74, 102, 114, 127, 132
Lincoln, Abraham
    16, 32, 48
Lowell, James Russell 62
Lubbock, Sir John 24
Lucius Annaeus Seneca
    106
Luther, Martin 89
MacDonald, George 55
Macaulay, Thomas 61
Marcus Aurelius 110, 136
Marshall, Catherine 15
Marshall, Peter 131
Martial 140, 142, 146
Masters, Edgar Lee 66
McEntire, Reba 72
Merton, Thomas 108
Meyer, F. B. 52
Milton, John 106
Montagu, Ashley 61
Montaigne 115, 126
More, Hannah 75
More, Sir Thomas 59
Moses, Grandma 22
Mother Teresa 79
Newman, John Henry,
    Cardinal 22
Niebuhr, Reinhold 77, 85
Ortega y Gasset 85

Parton, Dolly 142
Paul the Apostle 107
Pavlova, Anna 68
Peck, Scott 86
Petrarch 92
Pindar 18
Plato 62, 87, 143
Pope, Alexander 89
Pope John Paul II 65
Pope John XXIII 137
Rickey, Branch 123
Roosevelt, Eleanor
    99, 128
Roosevelt, Franklin D. 48
Royce, Josiah 139
Rosten, Leo 51
Rubinstein, Artur 22, 29
Ruskin, John 19, 37, 69
Russell, Bertrand 81
Ruth, Babe 123
Saint Francis of Assisi
    132
Sangster, Margaret 28
Schuller, Robert 100
Scott, Sir Walter 25, 59
Sheen, Fulton J. 147
Shellenberger, Dorothy
    51
Singer, Isaac Bashevis 37

Smuts, Jan 120
Socrates 20
St. John of the Cross 84
Steinbeck, John 25
Stevenson, R. L. 78
Swift, Jonathan 148
Swindoll, Charles 130
Tacitus 123
Tarfon, Rabbi 62
Tauler, Johannes 81, 108
Thackeray, William
    Makepeace 115
Thaxter, Celia 100
Thoreau, Henry David
    36, 140
Tolstoy, Leo 54, 94
Twain, Mark 122
Unamuno, Miguel de 131
Ustinov, Peter 89
Van Buren, Martin 69
Villa, Anthony Dalla 68
Walton, Sir John 56
Washington, Martha 76
Wayne, John 122
Wescott, Glenway 86
Whitman, Walt 48
Wilcox, Ella Wheeler 115
Wilder, Thornton 98
Wright, Frank Lloyd 99

About the Author

Criswell Freeman is a Doctor of Clinical Psychology who lives, writes and works in Nashville, Tennessee. Dr. Freeman is the author of numerous books, including *When Life Throws You a Curveball, Hit It* and The Wisdom Series from Walnut Grove Press. Freeman is also the host of *Wisdom Made in America*, a nationally syndicated radio program.

About the *God Can Handle It* Series

God Can Handle It is a series published by Brighton Books. Each title features inspirational quotations and relevant scripture passages. The series includes:

God Can Handle It
> by Jim Gallery

God Can Handle It... Day by Day
> by S. M. Henriques

Gad Can Handle It ... for Kids
> by S. M. Henriques

God Can Handle It...for Teenagers
> by Julie & Jim Gallery

God Can Handle It ...for Mothers
> by Carlene Ward

God Can Handle It ...for Fathers
> by Jim Gallery

God Can Handle It ... Marriage
> by S. M. Henriques

God Can Handle It ...for Graduates
> by Criswell Freeman

For more information, call 1-800-256-8584.